UNUSUAL FARM ANIMALS

RAISING
SNAILS

TANYA DELLACCIO

Jefferson Twp. Public Library
1031 Weldon Road
Oak Ridge, NJ 07438
973-208-6244
www.jeffersonlibrary.net

PowerKiDS press.

New York

Published in 2020 by The Rosen Publishing Group, Inc.
29 East 21st Street, New York, NY 10010

First Edition

Editor: Tanya Dellaccio
Book Design: Michael Flynn

Photo Credits: Cover (snails) Kostiantyn Kravchenko/Shutterstock.com; (series barn wood background) PASAKORN RANGSIYANONT/Shutterstock.com; (series wood frame) robert_s/Shutterstock.com; cover, pp. 1, 3, 23, 24 (snail icon) Maxim Gaigul/Shutterstock.com; p. 5 shoot4pleasure/Shutterstock.com; p. 6 scott conner/Shutterstock.com; p. 7 DR pics/Shutterstock.com; p. 9 MARCELLO PATERNOSTRO/AFP/Getty Images; p. 10 JANEK SKARZYNSKI/AFP/Getty Images; p. 11 Butus/Shutterstock.com; pp. 13, 17 BSIP/Universal Images Group/Getty Images; p. 15 (main) AFP/Getty Images; p. 15 (inset) Alexandr Jitarev/Shutterstock.com; p. 18 Foodpictures/Shutterstock.com; p. 19 shakim888/Shutterstock.com; p. 21 DNikolaev/Shutterstock.com; p. 22 Aleksandar Grozdanovski/Shutterstock.com.

Library of Congress Cataloging-in-Publication Data

Names: Dellaccio, Tanya.
Title: Raising snails / Tanya Dellaccio.
Description: New York : PowerKids Press, 2020. | Series: Unusual farm animals | Includes glossary and index.
Identifiers: ISBN 9781725309142 (pbk.) | ISBN 9781725309166 (library bound) | ISBN 9781725309159 (6 pack)
Subjects: LCSH: Snails–Juvenile literature.
Classification: LCC QL430.4 D45 2020 | DDC 594'.38–dc23

Manufactured in the United States of America

CPSIA Compliance Information: Batch #CWPK20. For Further Information contact Rosen Publishing, New York, New York at 1-800-237-9932.

CONTENTS

SMALL AND SIMPLE. 4

A SNAIL'S FAMILY 6

SMALL SPACES, SAFE SNAILS 8

THE BASICS 10

EASY EATING 12

BABY SNAILS 14

GROWING UP. 16

FANCY FOODS 18

SNAIL MAIL 20

SNAIL BEAUTY. 22

GLOSSARY 23

INDEX 24

WEBSITES 24

SMALL AND SIMPLE

People all around the world raise different kinds of animals on farms. Some people raise cows or chickens. Others raise bees. Some people even raise snails!

Even though these slow and slimy creatures don't seem like usual animals to raise on a farm, they're very popular! There are thousands of snail farms around the world. Snails are usually raised to be sold for food. The slime they make is also used for beauty **products**!

HOW UNUSUAL!

There are over 35,000 different **species** of land snails around the world!

SOME SNAIL SPECIES LIVE ON LAND, WHILE OTHERS LIVE IN THE WATER.

A SNAIL'S FAMILY

Snails are mollusks, which are animals that have a soft, squishy body and can live on land or in water. Mollusks are part of the gastropod class. This includes snails, which have outer shells, and slugs, which don't have shells.

SLUG

HOW UNUSUAL!

Species of mollusks differ greatly in size. Some can be tiny, weighing only 0.25 ounce (7 grams), while others can be huge—weighing around 450 pounds (204 kg)!

THE FAMILY HELICIDAE IS A LARGE GROUP OF LAND-LIVING, EDIBLE SNAILS. THE WORD "AGRICULTURE" MEANS FARMING. FARMING SNAILS IS CALLED HELICICULTURE.

Only certain species of snails can be raised on a farm. For starters, they need to be able to survive on land. Since not all snails are edible, or safe to eat, it's important to have snails that people can eat and will want to buy.

SMALL SPACES, SAFE SNAILS

Since snails are so small, they don't need much space to live and grow. The most important thing a farmer needs when building their snail pen is making sure it's enclosed, or closed off, enough so the snails can't escape.

The snails' home can be made of many different things, including wood or metal. The enclosure should be fenced and covered with netting to keep out predators. Snails sometimes eat dirt, making it important that their home has clean, healthy soil, too.

HOW UNUSUAL!

Snails like warm weather. About 70°Fahrenheit (21°Celsius) is ideal. If it's 45°F (7°C) or below, snails hibernate, or sleep for a long period of time! They do this every year during the winter months.

FARMERS CAN RAISE SNAILS INDOORS, TOO!

9

THE BASICS

Aside from the enclosures, snail farmers only need a few small tools to tend to their livestock. Basic gardening tools are necessary to keep the plants in the pen healthy and safe for the snails.

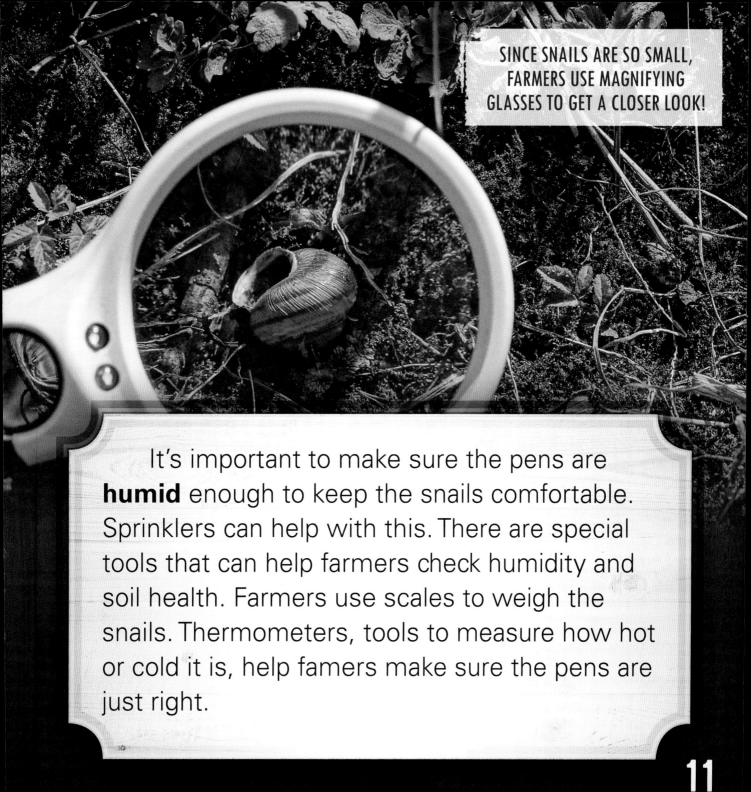

It's important to make sure the pens are **humid** enough to keep the snails comfortable. Sprinklers can help with this. There are special tools that can help farmers check humidity and soil health. Farmers use scales to weigh the snails. Thermometers, tools to measure how hot or cold it is, help famers make sure the pens are just right.

EASY EATING

Snails aren't picky eaters. They mostly eat plants and dirt. Farmers usually plant fruit and vegetable gardens in their snail pens. The snails will pick and choose what they want to eat from the garden.

Since snails like to dig, it's important to have soil that's healthy and has a lot of **nutrients**. When digging, snails eat the soil. Some soils have special **vitamins** and **minerals** in them that help snails grow. Snails also need plenty of water to survive.

HOW UNUSUAL!

Did you know that snails have teeth? They have thousands of teeny tiny teeth inside their jaws! Their teeth are strong, too.

A SNAIL HAS BETWEEN 2,000 AND 15,000
LITTLE TEETH INSIDE ITS MOUTH!

BABY SNAILS

Since snail farmers make the most money from selling snails for their meat, **mating** snails is an important part of farming them. Snails have both male and female parts, which means they can make babies with any snail of the same species.

A single snail can lay up to 100 eggs! They bury the eggs inside the dirt while the baby snails grow. Snail eggs take two to four weeks to **hatch**. After the snails hatch, farmers put the babies in a different enclosure.

HOW UNUSUAL!

Adult snails grow pointy little spikes. They shoot these spikes at the other snail before mating. The points are called "love darts"!

SNAIL EGGS

BABY SNAILS ARE BORN WITH SHELLS, BUT THOSE SHELLS ARE VERY WEAK AT FIRST.

GROWING UP

Newborn snails are hungry! They eat the egg they were hatched from to strengthen their body and shell.

It's very important to make sure the snails' new home isn't too hot or cold. If it isn't just right, the eggs won't hatch quickly enough. This could lead to baby snails eating the eggs of other snails waiting to hatch. After the baby snails are born, they take around one to two years to grow up.

HOW UNUSUAL!

Snails will eat just about anything if they're hungry enough. They've been known to chew through cardboard!

YOU CAN TELL IF A SNAIL IS FULL GROWN BY LOOKING AT ITS SHELL.

17

FANCY FOODS

When snails are full grown, they're ready to be sold for their meat. Farmers get them ready to sell and ship by separating the snails that they're selling. The snails need to have an empty stomach before they're sent off, so farmers give them nothing but water for seven or so days to clear out their bellies.

HOW UNUSUAL!

Some people even eat snail eggs! This dish is called snail caviar.

SNAIL CAVIAR

HAVE YOU EVER HEARD OF ESCARGOT? IT'S COOKED SNAIL! PEOPLE ALL AROUND THE WORLD ENJOY EATING THIS TASTY DISH. A VILLAGE IN FRANCE, WHERE THE DISH WAS CREATED, HAS AN EVENT EVERY YEAR DURING WHICH PEOPLE EAT AROUND 100,000 SNAILS!

Farmers sell snails all around the world to restaurants and chefs who cook the little creatures with different seasonings and sauces and serve them to people to eat.

SNAIL MAIL

Raising and selling snails isn't all easy. The little squishy slowpokes are considered agricultural pests. Since they eat pretty much anything, they can cause many problems if they escape in new areas.

The U.S. Department of Agriculture keeps track of where and how farmers ship snails. For example, snails are shipped in three separate boxes inside of each other, to make sure they don't eat through the box and escape. There's also a list of **precautions** farmers must take when building their snail farm. All farms must follow these rules.

SNAILS CAN SELL FOR AROUND $2 APIECE, DEPENDING ON THE AREA AND BUYER.

21

SNAIL BEAUTY

Snail farming is a growing business! Farmers are finding new ways to use snails, making farming them more profitable. Snail goods are becoming very popular in skin-care items. Beauty companies make masks and creams out of the snails' slime. It's known to make skin smoother and add moisture.

The snail farming business makes billions of dollars each year! As long as farmers follow the rules set in place for raising these unusual farm animals, snail farms will continue to **thrive**.

hatch: To break open or come out of.

humid: Having a lot of moisture in the air.

mate: To bring two animals together to make babies.

mineral: A naturally occurring solid matter that is not of plant or animal origin.

nutrient: Something taken in by a plant or animal that helps it grow and stay healthy.

precaution: A measure taken to prevent harm.

product: Something made from another thing.

species: A group of plants or animals that are all the same kind.

thrive: To grow successfully.

vitamin: A natural matter that is often in food and can help a body grow and stay healthy.

D
Department of Agriculture, U.S., 20

E
eggs, 14, 15, 16, 18
escargot, 19

H
heliciculture, 7
Helicidae, 7

L
land, 4, 5, 6, 7

M
meat, 14, 18

mollusks, 6

P
pens, 8, 10, 11, 12
plants, 10, 12

S
shells, 6, 15, 16, 17
slime, 4, 22
slugs, 6
soil, 8, 11, 12
species, 4, 5, 7

T
teeth, 12, 13

W
water, 5, 6, 12, 18

WEBSITES

Due to the changing nature of Internet links, PowerKids Press has developed an online list of websites related to the subject of this book. This site is updated regularly. Please use this link to access the list: www.powerkidslinks.com/ufa/snails